The Great
Chicago Fire

Essential Events

THE GREAT CHICAGO FIRE

BY L. L. OWENS

Content Consultant
Drew E. VandeCreek, Ph.D.
Director of Digital Projects
Northern Illinois University Libraries

ABDO
Publishing Company

CREDITS

Published by ABDO Publishing Company, 8000 West 78th Street, Edina, Minnesota 55439. Copyright © 2008 by Abdo Consulting Group, Inc. International copyrights reserved in all countries. No part of this book may be reproduced in any form without written permission from the publisher. The Essential Library-TM is a trademark and logo of ABDO Publishing Company.

Editor: Paula Lewis
Cover Design: Becky Daum
Interior Design: Lindaanne Donohoe

Library of Congress Cataloging-in-Publication Data
Owens, L. L.
  The great Chicago fire / L. L. Owens.
    p. cm. — (Essential events)
  Includes bibliographical references and index.
  ISBN 978-1-59928-851-2
  1. Great Fire, Chicago, Ill., 1871—Juvenile literature. 2. Fires—Illinois—Chicago—History—19th century—Juvenile literature. 3. Chicago (Ill.)—History—to 1875—Juvenile literature.
  I. Title.

F548.42.O96 2007
977.3'041—dc22

                                                        2007012007

TABLE OF CONTENTS

The O'Leary barn, where the Great Chicago Fire originated

THE MYTH OF
MRS. O'LEARY'S COW

On October 8, 1871, a fire that would destroy three square miles (8 sq km) of Chicago, Illinois, started on the city's West Side. It was late on a Sunday evening, and many people had already gone to bed assuming they would awaken to a typical

Monday morning. They could not have been more wrong. The city and its residents had to find a way to deal with a fire that was raging out of control. People were trying to save their homes and their lives—and fight the inferno that would be forever known as the Great Chicago Fire of 1871.

The blaze spread through Chicago from Sunday night until early Tuesday morning. When the fire finally died down, the city was in shock. Homes and businesses had been destroyed—not just a few, but entire blocks of buildings. Hundreds of lives had been lost. The devastation to the people, land, property, economy, and spirit would be felt for years.

Evidence showed that the blaze originated in a barn located at 137 DeKoven Street. That barn belonged to Patrick and Catherine "Kate" O'Leary. But how did the fire start? Was someone careless while smoking or using a candle? Did someone purposely try to destroy the O'Learys' property? Was it possible that lightning struck the barn on a clear night?

The Chicago Board of Police and Fire Commissioners began

"At 9:30 a small cow barn attached to a house on the corner of DeKoven and Jefferson streets, one block north of Twelfth street, emitted a bright light, followed by a blaze, and in a moment the building was hopelessly on fire."[1]

—*Chicago Tribune*

investigating the fire in November 1871. A committee was formed to conduct a formal inquiry. They questioned witnesses to the fire in its early stages and others who offered helpful information.

Although the committee took more than 1,000 pages of testimony from approximately 50 people, they were unable to establish the exact cause of the fire. The committee's report to the public, stated, in part,

> ... *whether it originated from a spark blown from a chimney on that windy night, or was set on fire by human agency, we are unable to determine.*[2]

Rumors Spread Like Fire

Despite the absence of an official cause, rumors about the fire were bound to spread from person to person all over town. And spread they did. Within hours, the most widespread rumor placed blame on a defenseless creature that simply could not speak for itself—Mrs. O'Leary's cow.

And, how could a cow start a fire? According to one rumor, at about nine o'clock on the night of the fire,

Mrs. O'Leary is sent sprawling while other livestock scatter in fright.

Kate O'Leary was in the family barn milking her cows. Her husband, Patrick, worked as a laborer, and Kate ran a milk route. The couple had recently prepared for the winter ahead by stocking the barn with coal and firewood, as well as a large supply of hay for the animals.

Legend says that Mrs. O'Leary finished up that night by milking a cow named Daisy. She placed a kerosene lantern on the ground next to the cow so she could see what she was doing. When Mrs. O'Leary went inside for the night, she accidentally left the lantern behind. Then Daisy kicked over the lantern. The glass lamp shattered, and the flame quickly spread from hay near Daisy's feet to the piles of hay in the barn. The coal and the firewood caught fire, too. Very quickly, the entire barn went up in flames. The windy night helped the blaze streak across the flat, dry land. The fire consumed everything in its path. What started as a small flame became a fire that was too big to hold back.

Some of Mrs. O'Leary's neighbors claimed that she

Mrs. O'Leary's Cow

An instrumental song called "Mrs. O'Leary's Cow" won a Grammy for songwriter Brian Wilson in 2004. Wilson was a founding member of the successful 1960s surfer rock group, The Beach Boys. He wrote the song, initially titled "Fire," in 1966 for a Beach Boys album called *Smile*. However, that album was never released in its original form.

Years later, Wilson decided to issue a reworked version of *Smile*. It included the song he now called "Mrs. O'Leary's Cow."

Wilson reflected on the process of recording the song in his book *Wouldn't It Be Nice: My Own Story*,

> The chords were weird ... twenty-four takes before I was satisfied. ... The weirdest was the crash and crackle of instruments smoldering for the final time. Listening to the playback, I began to feel unnerved by the music, strange and eerie. I liked the music. But it scared me.[3]

Wilson was further disturbed when he learned the building next to the Los Angeles recording studio he'd been working in had burned down the night after the recording session. Reportedly, an "unusual number of fires" broke out in Los Angeles over the next several days.

confessed to being in the barn when the fire started. They said that Mrs. O'Leary saw the cow kick over the lantern and then ran into the house. A few neighbors even claimed that they had found pieces of the lantern in the remains of the O'Leary barn. These neighbors, who claimed to be witnesses, gave conflicting information as to why Mrs. O'Leary was even in the barn at that time.

Years later, one young man gained a bit of attention with his recollection of the fire. As a young boy at the time of the fire, he had investigated the fire scene. He claimed to have found the broken lantern hidden under the floorboards at the barn site. However, there was no reason for the barn to have wooden floorboards and no way to explain why they had not burned. When the young man was asked to produce the broken lamp, he claimed that an Irish servant trying to cover up the "crime" had stolen it from him.

Most published reports, however, quote Mrs. O'Leary's testimony that she was in bed when the fire started. She testified that she had no knowledge of how or exactly when the fire started. No one was ever able to disprove any of her statements. Yet the myth of "Mrs. O'Leary's cow" persisted.

Structures large and small were reduced to rubble by the fire.

A Scapegoat

So what is the reason for the myth's popularity? First, it is a good story that is easy to remember. Secondly, it provided a possible answer to how the fire started—even though no eyewitness testimony was provided that could explain those first moments of ignition. Third, the myth offered the stunned city of Chicago a scapegoat. People wanted to understand why their city had burned and how the fire had started. The city needed someone to blame.

Mrs. O'Leary became the unfortunate scapegoat. In that era in Chicago, Catholics and immigrants were often treated unfairly and subjected to ridicule or other forms of bigotry. A common misconception of Irish immigrants depicted them as lazy, often drunk, and prone to poor judgment. In conversation and in the newspapers, Mrs. O'Leary was portrayed as a clumsy, unfortunate, unkempt woman whose drunken carelessness directly led to the fire. In reality, she was honest, proud, sober, and hardworking. She, like everyone else, had no idea how the fire started and was heartbroken by the destruction it caused.

Public attention focused on Mrs. O'Leary for quite a while after the fire. She suffered for it, too, as the unwilling target of many unflattering jokes, stories, and illustrations. For example, the *Chicago Times* hinted that she had vowed revenge after being kicked out of a financial aid program—suggesting that was why she had started the fire. The newspaper ignored the fact that Mrs. O'Leary had not been in the program.

In the early days after the tragedy, Mrs. O'Leary gave interviews trying to help. But journalists tended to twist her words and make fun of her accent, speech pattern, and appearance. She quickly decided to stay away from the press as much as possible.

Every year near the anniversary of the fire, reporters would show up on her doorstep wanting new quotes about the event. Every year, she would send them away with no comment.

Fifteen years after the fire, *The Chicago Daily News* ran a piece on the fire. Mrs. O'Leary refused to speak to the reporter, who then offered this hurtful description of his visit to the O'Leary home:

> *The house has no front door, in lieu of glass clothing is stuffed into two or three windows, and long before a stranger reaches the place the pungent odor of distillery swill and the effluvium of cows proclaim that old habits are strong with Mrs. O'Leary and that she is still in the milk business.* [4]

"Old Mother Leary" was a popular song in Chicago during the late nineteenth century. It became so well known that it likely helped fuel the myth that Mrs. O'Leary and her cow were responsible for the fire. It certainly helped to keep the legend of Mrs. O'Leary and her cow alive. The song is also known by the alternate titles "Mrs. O'Leary's Cow" and "There'll Be a Hot Time in the Old Town Tonight." Following is a common version of the lyrics. It is fairly fun and lighthearted—unless you are Kate O'Leary.

Original Version

Late one night
When we were all in bed
Old Mother Leary
Left a lantern in the shed
And when the cow kicked it over
She winked her eye and said,
"There'll be a hot time
In the old town, tonight!"
Spoken:
FIRE! FIRE! FIRE![5]

THE MYTH SEEMS "TRUE" WITH TIME

Unfortunately, the subject of the fire was a constant source of pain and distress for Mrs. O'Leary. Her husband, Patrick, passed away in 1894. After 24 years as a recluse, Mrs. O'Leary died on July 4, 1895. She died having endured public scorn for nearly a quarter of a century.

By the fortieth anniversary of the fire, "Mrs. O'Leary" had become a quaint mythical figure in

Chicago's history. Time helped put some distance between the awful effects of the fire and the daily lives of those who lived in Chicago. With time, the city of Chicago had healed and Mrs. O'Leary's place in history began to change.

Events in the city marking the fortieth anniversary of the fire included a parade through downtown Chicago. Actors played the roles of the O'Learys and there was a stand-in for Daisy the cow. A plump, merry "Kate" wore a long, white apron and flower-topped hat. She carried a large, silver milk bucket and happily led "Daisy" on the parade route. A stately looking "Patrick" casually walked behind the two stars of the show. By this time, the long-held dislike for the O'Learys had given way to a more cheerful attitude toward the primary characters in the legend surrounding one of Chicago's most important moments.

Embraced as folklore in American culture well into the twentieth century, the story was told in many ways. In 1935, acclaimed American artist Norman Rockwell painted a tribute to the legend, titled *Milking Daisy*. The artwork shows a plump, smiling Mrs. O'Leary milking a cow that is gazing at the viewer over its backside. A lantern is placed at the cow's feet. In 1938, Alice Brady won the Academy Award for Best Supporting Actress

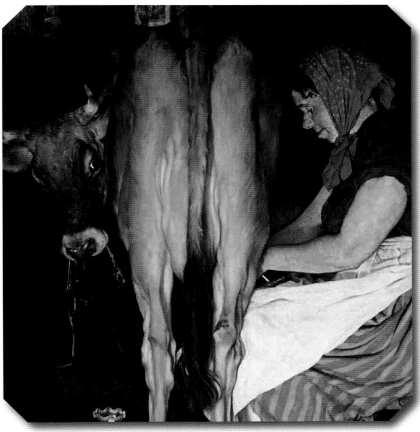

Artist Norman Rockwell's portrayal of Daisy and Kate O'Leary

for her portrayal of Mrs. O'Leary in the movie *In Old Chicago*. The film depicts a fictionalized version of the fire presenting Mrs. O'Leary as a widowed laundress. The story includes Daisy the cow kicking over a lantern, but that is about the only detail that matches the legend of the fire.

The theme for the 1960 Rose Bowl Parade was "Tall Tales and True." Chicago submitted a float with a design

Chicago's City Council passed a resolution in October 1997 that cleared Mrs. O'Leary and her cow of any responsibility for the Great Chicago Fire of 1871.

featuring a model of the burning O'Leary barn and a cow made of carnations and chrysanthemums.

It is difficult to say whether Kate O'Leary would have enjoyed the positive attention she received in later years. Surely she would have been comforted to learn that history has been kind to her.

Modern scholars have completely cleared her of causing the biggest disaster in Chicago history. And the facts speak clearly to the reality that—cow or no cow, lantern or no lantern—in the fall of 1871, Chicago was destined to burn down sooner or later.

The City That a Cow Kicked Over was published ten years after the fire. This nursery rhyme describes the events of the fire.

A depiction of the Chicago area in the early 1800s

Chicago Before the Fire

The first recorded history of the Chicago area comes from 17th century European explorers. Native Americans had inhabited and hunted the land for hundreds of years. The area eventually attracted settlers from other lands.

European Discovery

In 1673, noted explorers Jacques Marquette and Louis Jolliet surveyed the area that would eventually become Chicago, Illinois. Marquette, a Frenchman, was a Jesuit missionary. The French-Canadian Jolliet was a fur trader. Along with five other explorers, the two had been sent on an expedition by the governor of New France, Quebec. The purpose of the journey was to find the Northwest Passage, a waterway shortcut through the New World to the Indies. The government that found the passage could claim the right to control its traffic and import goods straight from Asian markets. This would not only open up a vast new market for commerce, but whoever controlled the passage could profit greatly.

Marquette and Jolliet discovered the Chicago area with help from Native Americans they befriended. The men soon realized that they had not found the Northwest Passage. However, they did understand the value of the area. Marquette and Jolliet recognized the great potential in the land and its location between

The Beginning of a Town

Chicago was incorporated as a town in the summer of 1833. At the time, it covered an area of about three-eighths of a square mile (1 sq km).

the Chicago and Des Plaines Rivers. The Chicago River flowed into Lake Michigan. The Des Plaines River connected to the Mississippi River. This access to major waterways meant that the area could easily become a hub for transportation and trade.

The Algonquian Indian name for the area was *Chigagou*. The name's meaning has been debated. Many historians believe that it meant "onion field" due to the odor of the wild onions or garlic that grew in the swampy area. Other translations include "skunk," "strong," and "powerful."

In 1696, French Jesuits built the Mission of the Guardian Angel hoping to convert the American Indians to Christianity. For a long time, the primary tribes were the Miami, Sauk, and Fox. Trappers and traders visited into the 1700s. But by the mid-18th century, the Pottawatomie tribe had taken control of the land.

EARLY SETTLEMENT

The first non-native settler in Chicago was Jean Baptiste Point du Sable. He was a French African from Haiti who was the son of a wealthy French merchant. In the 1770s, he built a perma-nent settlement on the banks of the Chicago River

Jean Baptiste Point du Sable

near what is now the Michigan Avenue Bridge. Skilled in many trades, he worked as a miller, cooper, and carpenter. He took a Pottawatomie bride and became a vital part of Chicago's early history. Records show that Chicago's first trial, first marriage ceremony, and first election all were held at the home of Jean Baptiste Point du Sable.

Under the terms of the Treaty of Greenville, the United States used the area surrounding Chicago as a military post beginning in 1795. Fort Dearborn was built in 1803. And in 1816, the United States won part of the land from the Pottawatomie, Ojibwa, and Ottawa tribes with the Treaty of St. Louis. Illinois became the nation's twenty-first state in 1818.

By the mid-1820s, Chicago had become a major western destination and remained a busy trading post. Native Americans ceded the rest of the surrounding area in the Treaty of Chicago. On August 12, 1833, Chicago was incorporated as a town with 350 residents. Nearly four years later, Chicago's population had increased to 4,170. Chicago was officially incorporated as a city on March 4, 1837. Influential businessman William B. Ogden was elected Chicago's first mayor in May of that year.

The city was primed for growth. In the coming decades, railroads arrived and turned Chicago into the transportation hub of the United States. The city's population exploded. In 1860, the city hosted the Republican National Convention. This convention resulted in the nomination of presidential candidate Abraham Lincoln. By 1870, one year before the Great Fire, about 300,000 people called Chicago home.

QUEEN OF THE WEST

Chicago had enjoyed an expanding population, economy, and reputation in the years before the Great Fire. Known as the "Queen of the West," Chicago attracted immigrants by the thousands each year. A constant flow of settlers and visitors arrived by wagon, ship, or train. Ten railroads converged in the city.

People saw Chicago as a city of great opportunity. Many East Coast merchants, tradesmen, and business people scrambled to take advantage of the growth by opening new businesses.

Located on the southwestern shores of Lake Michigan, Chicago grew into a city of distinct neighborhoods and divisions. The Chicago River divided the city into the North, South, and West Sides. The business district flourished in the central district.

The lumber business boomed. Homes, warehouses, grain elevators, storefronts, churches, and stockyards could not be built fast enough. They were built quickly, however, and often cheaply.

Queen of the West

Not long after its incorporation, Chicago became a major U.S. city. In 1840, it was number 92 on the list of largest cities in the United States. It moved up to number nine on the list within 20 years and was known as the Queen of the West.

At the time of the Great Fire, the city was barely 40 years old and supported more than 1,100 factories!

A City Ready to Burn

In October 1871, piles of lumber were stacked up in the streets for the next building project. Wood seemed to be everywhere, and not just as the main building material for the city's tens of thousands of buildings. Chicago had 88 miles (142 km) of paved streets—of which 57 miles (92 km) were paved with pine. There were 561 miles (903 km) of wooden sidewalks. Chicago was a city of wood buildings and wood streets. The city truly was ready to burn. After the fire, the *Chicago Daily Tribune* and the

---

Two Days, Two Fires

Victims of the Great Fire that started on October 8 shared memories of feeling fortunate that the terrible West Side fire on October 7th had not affected them. Mabel McIlvaine collected such experiences in her 1915 book, *Reminiscences of Chicago During the Great Fire.*

Chicago landscape architect H. W. S. Cleveland said, "On the night of Saturday, October 7th, there was a great fire on the West Side, of which we saw the light; and on Sunday morning I took my early walk to the ruins and brought back the Sunday *Tribune* containing an account of the "Great Fire," and at breakfast we were discussing it as a terrible calamity, little dreaming how soon it would sink into insignificance in comparison with the destruction which followed."[1]

Mrs. Alfred Hebard and her family were passing through Chicago that fateful weekend. She recalled a similar reaction to news of the fire.

"All through the weary hours of October 8, 1871, we were enjoying pleasant anticipation of the rest and comfort so sure to be found at the Palmer House. ... as we walked to church, my husband remarked, 'How fortunate that the fire was last night instead of to-day.'"[2]

They had no way of knowing what the evening of October 8 would bring!

Chicago Journal of Commerce commented on the inevitability of such a catastrophe. They cited the dry weather and the city's construction material as prime clues that something horrible would happen.

An article in the *Journal of Commerce* set the scene,

> *For nearly fifteen weeks there had not fallen enough rain to penetrate the earth one full inch. … the city was heated, dry, and parched. Indeed, all through the West, fires were devastating extensive forests and destroying ripening crops, driving frontier settlers from their cabins and even overwhelming entire villages. For days, the prevailing at-mosphere of our city seemed ready to kindle into a blaze.[3]*

The *Chicago Daily Tribune* pointed out,

> *In a city where time was everything, and durability was not a matter much considered, street after street was lined with wooden buildings, not with oaken beams and floorings, but an aggregation of flimsily constructed and inflammable pine.[4]*

Building Standards

Chicago was one of the fastest growing cities. Unfortunately, too many buildings were not built to standards. Some Chicago buildings, including the Courthouse, were considered fireproof. But for the most part—even with certain prominent features made of marble or stone—the buildings had wooden frames and wood-carved decorations that had been painted to look like stonework.

Playing With Fire

Chicago residents "played with fire" as part of their everyday lives. They had to. Fire was used to cook their food, heat and light their homes, and light the streets.

It is not surprising that accidental fires frequently started. Chicago experienced about two fires every day. It was common to hear a fire alarm.

Chicago suffered dozens of fires in the spring and summer of 1871. Firemen responded to 20 fires during the first week of October. On October 7, just one day before the Great Fire, a fire destroyed four square blocks on the West Side. On October 8, the *Chicago Daily Tribune* printed this report:

The sounding of the fire alarm from Box No. 248, at about 11 o'clock last night, was the solemn prelude to one of the most disastrous and imposing conflagrations which has ever visited a city which has already enrolled in her annals numbers of such visitations, many of them so terrible that they can serve as eras in her history. For days past, alarm has followed alarm, but the comparatively trifling losses have familiarized us to the pealing of the Court House bell, and we had forgotten that the absence of rain for three weeks had left everything so dry and inflammable a condition that a spark might start a fire which would sweep from end to end of the city.[5]

The alarm box that failed. On the evening of October 8, local residents turned in an alarm right away, but the message never made it to the Courthouse.

Carrying what they could, residents fled the city.

THE GREAT CONFLAGRATION

he Great Chicago Fire of 1871 began late the evening of Sunday, October 8, and persisted until the early morning of Tuesday, October 10. It started in the O'Leary barn and was fanned by a wind from the southwest. Before it ended, the inferno traveled an astonishing four and a half miles (7.3 km) to the northern tip of the city.

Damage from the fire was so great that the event was one of the biggest U.S. disasters of the nineteenth century. The Great Chicago Fire—also known as the Great Conflagration—unfolded across the city in just a few short days. The fallout, however, would have lasting effects on the great city of Chicago.

Sunday, October 8

Between eight-thirty and nine o'clock Sunday night, the fire started at 137 DeKoven Street in Patrick and Kate O'Leary's barn. A guard keeping watch over the city from the Courthouse tower reported the fire

Safe

Even though the fire began in the O'Learys' barn, their cottage survived the fire.

but misidentified the location. The O'Learys lived near the intersection of DeKoven and Jefferson, but the guard reported the fire's location at Canalport and Halsted.

A shopkeeper noticed the fire and tried to activate a nearby alarm. The fire alarm box was new, but the alarm did not work. The fire rapidly jumped from one small wooden cottage to the next in the O'Learys' crowded neighborhood.

A *Chicago Evening Post* reporter gave his initial impressions of the scene:

> *I was at the scene in a few minutes. ... The land was thickly studded with one-story frame dwellings, cow stables, pig sties, corncribs, sheds innumerable; every wretched building within four feet of its neighbor, and everything of wood.*[1]

By ten o'clock, seven local fire companies had arrived to fight the fire. The blaze had been burning for almost 90 minutes and was already wildly out of control. People fled their homes as the fire quickly spread. Soon, eyewitnesses were shocked to see the flames cross the southern part of the Chicago River. Oil and debris floated on the water's surface, creating an easy path for the flames to follow to the other side. Businesses on the riverbanks included wooden warehouses and lumberyards. They were no match for the fire. At around midnight, the Gasworks exploded.

MONDAY, OCTOBER 9

The fire ravaged an area called Conley's Patch, killing many people who did not have time to leave their homes. Conley's Patch was a poor section of town and most of its inhabitants were Irish immigrants.

Courthouse officials released prisoners as the stately

building burned. The city had boasted that the building was nearly fireproof, but this fire overtook almost everything in its path.

The seemingly unstoppable fire continued to spread. Soon it crossed the State Street Bridge and made its way to the city's North Side.

One tourist visiting Chicago with her family described the terror she experienced as she tried to stay ahead of the flames:

> Our boys ran at full speed, and we followed, crossing State Street Bridge amid a shower of coals. ... The crowd thickened every moment; women with babies and bundles, men with kegs of beer—all jostling, scolding, crying, or swearing.[2]

Wrong Information

The guard who reported the fire quickly realized that he had given the wrong location. He asked to send out a corrected report. The telegraph operator, however, refused. He reasoned that a different report would only confuse the issue.

This error caused a significant delay in the efforts of the fire fighters and is a major reason that the blaze was not contained. The best time to control a fire is as it is taking hold. The Chicago firemen did not have that opportunity.

The woman's story was far from unique. As the fire gained strength and spread from block to block, frightened citizens had to make quick decisions. Many people jumped from upper-floor windows of burning buildings. Some survived their falls; others did not.

Firefighters battling the Great Fire

At one o'clock Monday morning, the new Palmer House Hotel was destroyed. And before two o'clock, as the fire moved east, Chicago lost both the Courthouse and the Sherman House hotel to the unstoppable flames. The heart of the city was gone.

Chicago Tribune editor-in-chief Horace White watched as the Courthouse caught fire. He said,

> *As the flames had leaped a vacant space of nearly two hundred feet to get at [the courthouse] roof, it was evident that most of the business portion of the city must go down.*[3]

Around this time, Chicago's mayor, Roswell Mason, sent word that the city was in trouble. He issued telegrams to the president of the United States and to Lieutenant General Philip Sheridan of the U.S. Army. He asked Sheridan to send troops to help fight the fires and keep the peace.

The fire crossed the Chicago River again after two o'clock and continued eastward for several hours, sweeping through the North Side, then the South Side. It greatly damaged the Waterworks, contaminating Chicago's drinking water—and effectively ending the firefighting efforts.

Traffic jams on the few remaining streets consisted of hordes of people, either on foot or in horse-drawn wagons, trying to reach safety. They carried all the possessions they possibly could. Some still had furniture and trunks of clothes. Others had nothing but the clothes on their backs. Those on the run had almost certainly lost their homes to the flames. Many had lost children, husbands, mothers, and friends.

Later, survivors noted some of the items people saved in this time of

Fleeing the Fire

After spending an entire day trying to outrun the fire, exhausted residents abandoned their few remaining possessions. They had to lessen their loads to keep going.

Some buried their most cherished items in the dirt to keep them safe. They hoped to be able to find them again later.

crisis. One woman clung to an expensive party gown. A man cradled pieces of a broken chair. A young girl clutched a stack of books. And one gentleman wandered the streets carrying nothing but two turnips.

The relentless inferno continued to chase people out of their homes and neighborhoods for hours. Some fled toward Lake Michigan and waded into the water, while others ventured away from the city and into the surrounding plains.

Fannie Belle Becker, who was ten at the time of the fire, later recalled that:

the heat was so in-tense that it drove us down to the water's Edge. ... we sat

The Peshtigo Fire

As Chicago fought its fire, the worst forest fire in North American history was in progress 240 miles (386 km) to the north.

The Peshtigo, Wisconsin area had an unusually hot and dry fall in 1871. In a "slash and burn" land-clearing method, some trees and vegetation were intentionally cut and burned. This proved dangerous after months without rain. Several small fires had started on October 8, but a cyclonic storm turned the small fires into one huge fire. The one horse-drawn water pump was of little use.

The burning forest bordered Peshtigo. The wooden buildings and sidewalks trapped residents. The fire leveled the town in about an hour. It spread across approximately 1.5 million acres (607,000 ha). Finally, heavy rains fell and the fire was extinguished.

The Peshtigo Fire was the deadliest fire in American history. It caused millions of dollars worth of damage and killed an estimated 1,200 to 2,500 people. Due to its remote location, it received much less news coverage than the Great Chicago Fire.

there until I was almost blind with the dirt and cinders that filled the air.[4]

Between six and eight o'clock that morning, William Ogden's lumberyard near the river burned. Soon the flames engulfed the Illinois Central Railroad and the McCormick Reaper Works.

Death and Destruction

The Great Chicago Fire killed 300 people. It destroyed nearly $200 million in property, and left more than 100,000 people homeless.

Horrific scenes played out until midmorning on Monday. The people of Chicago had been running for their lives for more than 12 hours. Lieutenant General Sheridan stepped in to help the city. By noon on Monday, October 9, Sheridan arranged for the homes and other buildings on Michigan Avenue to be blown up. The hope was that this would slow the fire and keep it from moving past this point. But this tactic did not work. The fire had a life of its own, and it seemed impossible to fight the flames.

The fire continued burning on the North Side of town through Monday evening. Many people had been running from the fire nonstop since the night before.

The front page of that day's *Evening Journal* featured an overview of the fire in headline size type. The gravity of the situation was evident in every line.

THE GREAT CALAMITY OF THE AGE!

Chicago in Ashes!!

Hundreds of Millions of Dollars' Worth of
Property Destroyed.

The South, the North and a Portion of the West
Divisions of the City in Ruins.

All the Hotels, Banks, Public Buildings,
Newspaper Offices and Great Business Blocks
Swept Away.

The Conflagration Still in Progress.

Fury of the Flames. [5]

On Monday night, the weather turned in Chicago's favor. A cold, hard rain fell on the still-burning city. Thousands of displaced citizens cheered and gave thanks despite being unable to take cover.

TUESDAY, OCTOBER 10

On Tuesday morning, October 10, emergency relief began arriving in Chicago. Wagon loads of basic supplies such as food, water, blankets, and clothing arrived from surrounding cities that had heard news of the fire. Weary Chicago was grateful for the help.

Newsboy with poster announcing the Chicago Fire

The rain had quieted most of the flames overnight, but what was left of the city still smoldered. The entire area was too hot and too dangerous to access. This frustrated the residents who wanted to visit their home

Waterworks

The fire damaged the city's Waterworks. Not only was this the main source for drinking water, but it was also the source of water for the firefighters. With the Waterworks shut down, people hauled water in buckets from the Chicago River and Lake Michigan to fight the fire.

sites. They would have to wait until it was safe to pick through the rubble in hopes of finding mementos of their former lives.

The next chapter of life in Chicago would be difficult. Hundreds of people had died and thousands had been ruined financially. People had lost their homes, their belongings, their jobs—they would have to start over. But first, they needed to share the news and their stories with each other and the rest of the world. ⌒

Residents flee the fires carrying others as well as treasured items.

The Chicago business district goes up in flames.

From the Eyes of the Fire

n 1871, Alexander Graham Bell was still
four years away from inventing the
telephone, a device that would revolutionize the world
of communication. At the time of the Great Fire,
Chicago residents could not easily communicate with

others. People received their news by word of mouth, printed newspapers, and handwritten personal letters. These methods were slow and took time.

However, news of the fire spread quickly through telegrams. As soon as the mayor sent telegrams for help, the telegraph wires were flooded with messages reaching out all over the country. The fire made national news, and people all over the United States followed the story. Those with friends and family who lived through the nightmarish disaster waited for letters to arrive. They waited for weeks and even months to get specific news, hoping to hear that their loved ones had survived the fire. The entire nation was concerned about the welfare of the Queen of the West and its residents. Newspapers reported the story and help came from other states as well as England and France. Donations of money, clothing, and food were gratefully accepted.

Excerpts from several harrowing eyewitness accounts featured in newspapers, memoirs, and personal letters have survived. Many of these accounts were collected by

"What a sight: a sea of fire, the heavens all ablaze, the air filled with burning embers, the wind blowing fiercely and tossing fire brands in all directions, thousands upon thousands of people rushing frantically about, burned out of shelter, without food, the rich yesterday poor today, destruction everywhere—is it not awful? It makes me sick. One could but exclaim: 'My God, when will it end?'"[1]

—*Jonas Hutchinson*

the Chicago Historical Society. These historical records make it possible for modern readers to see the horrors of the fire through the victims' eyes.

Chicago attorney Jonas Hutchinson had an office on Washington Street. He sent news to his mother in New Hampshire on October 9. Knowing she would be worried, he wanted to reassure her that he was safe. His words conveyed the heartbreak he and the citizens of Chicago felt for their ruined city.

Hutchinson wrote,

> *This has been an eventful day. Last night … a fire broke out here and from that time to this it has raged fearfully. We are in ruins. All the business portion of the city has fallen prey to the fiery fiend. Our magnificent streets for acres and acres lined with elegant structures are a heap of sightless rubbish. It cannot be described. One needs to see the wreck to appreciate it and then he cannot believe such havoc could be wrought in so short a time.* [2]

Mrs. Alfred Hebard and her family had stopped in Chicago on their way from Connecticut to their home in Iowa. They stayed at the Palmer House, something they did quite often during their travels. Mrs. Hebard recalled the mood at the hotel, as well as the scene outside, just after she heard the deadly fire was spreading.

Mrs. Hebard said,

> *Within the house the perfect quiet had astonished us—every man taking care of his own, silently and rapidly, few words being spoken. ... Outside we found confusion. Irish women with beds upon their shoulders crying noisily; children following as best they might; and all going—they knew not whither—only away from their burning homes.* [3]

Hutchinson wrote another letter to his mother on October 10. He was reeling from the day's events and could not sleep. He described the scope of the fire:

> *Tonight I am sitting up and I must tell you more about our great calamity. ... Two hundred millions of property have been destroyed. ... One hundred thousand people are homeless and the greater portion of them paupers. Only one house stands in the entire North Division and one also in the South Division. ... The fire extended 5 miles north and south and 2/3 of the way east and west and mind you, it missed nothing in its march.* [4]

Hutchinson also said that police were doing their best to keep order. There was so much looting and unruly behavior that police officers were given the go-ahead to shoot any man acting suspicious and refusing to speak when spoken to. Several men were shot, and

Looters breaking open barrels of liquor in a burned-out saloon

several others were "hung to lamp posts" by officers following orders.

Mary Fales also sent word to her mother on October 10. Mary and her husband David lived about three miles (5 km) northeast of the O'Leary barn. She wrote that by two o'clock on the morning of October 9, they knew the fire would reach their neighborhood. No one was safe.

Mrs. Fales had only minutes to gather what she most valued. With a few belongings, the Fales left their home and joined others on the crowded streets. Mrs. Fales wrote:

Questions

The most frequently asked questions among people on the streets during the fire were:
- ❖ Are you burned out?
- ❖ What did you save?
- ❖ Where are you going?

> *I cannot convey to you the way the streets looked. Everybody was out of their houses without one exception, and the sidewalks were covered with furniture and bundles of every description. The middle of the street was a jam of carts, carriages, wheel-barrows, and every sort of vehicle, and many horses being led along, all excited and prancing, some running away, I scarcely dared look right or left as I kept my seat by holding tightly to the trunk. The horse would not be restrained and I had to use all my powers to keep on. I was glad to go fast, for the fire behind us raged and crackled, and the whole earth, or all we saw of it was a lurid yellowish red.[5]*

Mrs. Aurelia King lived on Rush Street near Erie. Her husband Henry was a clothing merchant. She wrote to friends on October 21 to tell them about her experience fleeing the Great Fire. She and her family left their home at around two o'clock in the morning of October 9. She said:

You could not conceive anything more fearful. The wind was like a tornado, and I held fast to my little ones, fearing they would be lifted from my sight. ... truly I thought the day of judgment had come. I wish I could give you an adequate idea of that flight, but it is impossible. The streets were full of wagons trans– porting household furniture, people carrying on their backs the little bundles they had saved. ... It was only by some look of the eye or some motion [that] we

Human Nature: The Good and the Bad

The Great Fire brought out the best and the worst in people. With the city in flames, frightened residents fought for their lives and possessions. It was difficult and stressful, and there was no end in sight. Understandably, people felt helpless.

Many people reacted by thinking about others. Firemen watched their own homes burn while they fought to save the lives and property of others. In this difficult time, many citizens reached out to help each other.

Neighbors worked together in the chaos. Older children separated from their own families re-united terrified younger children with desperate parents. Strangers provided first aid for those who had been injured or burned, ripping up their own clothing to create a sling or bandage.

Sadly, though, some people stole food from their neighbors or looted burning businesses. Stunned witnesses reported dreadful acts such as men hijacking wagons and stealing horses by pulling riders to the ground. Others saw blankets grabbed from cold children, bread snatched from the elderly, and barrels of liquor opened and looted in the burned-out saloons.

could recognize friends—we were all so
blackened with dust and smoke. The
ladies, many of them, [were] dressed in
a nightgown and slippers. … Half of the
gentlemen were in nightshirts and
pantaloons.[6]

Losses

Reports in personal letters say that the Courthouse was destroyed in 20 minutes. A row of 40 houses burned to the ground in just 7 minutes.

Recalling what she saw upon fleeing her North Dearborn house with her husband, Anna Higginson wrote to an acquaintance:

… no words can give an idea of the horror of that night. …
it was not a flame but a solid wall of fire. … The air was full
of cinders; pieces of blazing shingles and boards and great
strips of tarred felt fell in every direction, now on the roofs
of houses yet unburned and then on the loads of furniture
and bedding which people were trying to save and which
they were continually obliged to abandon in the street in
order to save themselves.[7]

PRESERVING HISTORY

Chicago Tribune editor Horace White wrote a letter to
the editor of the *Cincinnati Commercial*. White stressed
the importance of recording personal accounts of the
fire so that future generations would know what had

happened. His letter ran in October 1871. White wrote in part:

> *The history of the Great Fire in Chicago which rises to the dignity of a national event, cannot be written until each witness, who makes any record whatever, shall have told what he saw. Nobody could see it all—no more than one man could see the whole of the Battle of Gettysburg. It was too vast, too swift, too full of smoke, too full of danger, for anybody to see it all. My experience derives its only public importance from the fact that what I did … a hundred thousand others did or attempted—that is, saved, or sought to save, their lives and enough of their wearing apparel to face the sky in.*[8]

All those who spoke to the press, sent personal letters to loved ones or recorded their memoirs of the fire. This greatly helped to preserve the history of the Great Chicago Fire for future generations.

Family trying to escape the fire by climbing onto a roof

The waterworks and the water tower, though damaged, survived the fire.

LANDMARKS AND BUSINESSES

The Great Conflagration turned Chicago to ashes, destroying many of the city's most important landmarks and businesses. The following Chicago landmarks were all damaged by the blaze.

GASWORKS

The Gasworks, which supplied the natural gas needed for gaslight, exploded in the early hours of Monday morning. That explosion helped transform the fire into the dangerous inferno that ravaged the city.

WATERWORKS

Most of the city relied on the Waterworks for its water supply. If the roof of the supply station had not caught fire that day, most of Chicago may have been saved. The roof was meant to be a temporary structure. Plans for a fireproof roof were under way. With the Waterworks on fire, the city's water supply was cut off, destroying the hope of putting out the fire.

"The fire, meanwhile, was coming nearer, and just as we began in earnest to pack. ... the Gasworks were destroyed and candles had to be resorted to."[1]

—*Palmer House guest Mrs. Alfred Hebard*

COURTHOUSE

Survivors of the Great Fire remembered the warning sound of the great bronze courthouse bell. It rang for five hours straight in the early hours of the ordeal. During the

The courthouse after the fire

fire, the center of the building burned through, causing the bell to drop from its tower through the floors to the courthouse basement.

TRIBUNE BUILDING

During the late nineteenth century, Chicago was a

major publishing city. The Great Fire reportedly destroyed up to 85 newspaper and publishing offices. The largest of these was the Tribune Building, home of the *Chicago Tribune*.

The stunning Tribune Building was built in 1869 for approximately $225,000. Considered fireproof, the building had no fire insurance. The building featured brick walls and iron beams, but the roof was made of wood and topped with new tar.

Firefighting efforts included keeping the roof wet, but it was impossible to stop the fire. The blaze gutted the building, leaving behind the contents of the fireproof vault, which included a box of matches.

The *Chicago Tribune* staff quickly set up makeshift offices. Within two days they were able to continue reporting on the disaster which included the destruction of their own building.

CROSBY'S OPERA HOUSE

Crosby's Opera House first opened its doors in 1865. It was a popular entertainment venue for locals and tourists. In the summer of 1871, owner Albert Crosby spent approximately $80,000 on plush new carpets, imposing bronze statues, grand mirrors, folding iron seats, and luxurious upholstery. The opera house was scheduled to reopen on October 9. The fire leveled it at about five o'clock that morning.

Too Many Losses to Count

The damage to Chicago during the Great Fire was monumental. In addition to homes, landmarks, and businesses, thousands of other structures were erased from the face of the city.

Five of Chicago's 17 grain elevators were completely destroyed. Approximately half of the corn and grain survived. Luckily, that was enough to help meet Chicago's needs right after the fire.

All 17 beer breweries burned to the ground. Many were connected to icehouses, stables, and cooper-and-blacksmith shops. Total damage to the breweries was estimated at more than $2 million.

City Hall and all banks (with the exception of their vaults), libraries, law offices, and primary telegraph offices were destroyed by the flames. Those losses included loan papers, mortgages, books, and legal decrees.

The coal yards sustained massive fire damage, leaving the city short on fuel for the winter.

The city also lost schools, churches, police stations, restaurants, tunnels, printing houses, bridges, fire engines, fire hydrants, and more.

Field, Leiter & Co.

Twentieth-century department store giant Marshall Field & Company began as a small Chicago dry goods store in 1852. First named P. Palmer & Co., it changed ownership a few times. By 1871, it was known as Field, Leiter & Co.

The store sat at the corner of Washington and State Streets. With its marble front, the store was nicknamed the "Marble Palace." The store perished in the fire.

LINCOLN PARK

This historic area started out as a cemetery and was dedicated as Lake Park by the Chicago City Council in 1864. After the 1865 assassination of President Abraham Lincoln, it was renamed Lincoln Park.

Situated on the Lake Michigan shore, the park drew thousands of residents fleeing the fire on October 9, 1871. For a time, it was one of the few safe gathering places in the city.

Wedding Gift

In 1871, Businessman Potter Palmer built the elaborate Palmer House Hotel as a wedding present to his bride, Bertha Honoré.

HOTELS

The beautiful Palmer House Hotel was located at the corner of State and Monroe Streets. It opened 13 days before it was reduced to rubble by the fire.

Other grand Chicago hotels destroyed in the fire included the Briggs House, Metropolitan House, Sherman House, St. James Hotel, Tremont House, Matteson House, and Grand Pacific Hotel.

BRIDGES

The Wells, Clark, State, and Rush Bridges connected Chicago's North Side and South Side. All of these bridges were destroyed.

Built in 1865, the Randolph Street Bridge provided an escape route. The bridge saved thousands of lives during the fire.

Chicago Evening Post reporter Joseph Edgar Chamberlin wrote,

> A torrent of humanity was pouring over the bridge. The Madison Street Bridge had long before become impassable. Drays, express wagons, trucks, and conveyances of every conceivable species and size crowded across in indiscriminate haste. Collisions happened almost every moment, and when one overloaded wagon broke down, there were enough men on hand to drag it and its contents over the bridge.[2]

Fleeing the Fire

The terror felt by the thousands of people who fled the fire via the Randolph Street Bridge was captured in a famous Currier and Ives lithograph titled *The Rush for Life Over the Randolph Street Bridge (Chicago in Flames).*

Crowds of people trying to cross the Randolph Street Bridge to escape the fire

A sketch of a broken oil lamp found in the O'Leary barn after the fire

INVESTIGATING THE CAUSE

Six weeks after the fire, Chicago authorities began their official investigation into the fire that destroyed their city. They recorded testimony from 49 witnesses, hoping to find the answers to how the fire started and why it was not contained early on.

The November 24 *Chicago Tribune* reported,

> *The Board of Police and Fire Commissioner Chadwick commenced, yesterday, the investigation into the origin of the fire, and its progress, with a view to place the responsibility upon whom it belongs.*[1]

On November 27, just a few days into the inquiry, the newspaper indicated that so far the investigation had not provided answers. The article stated,

> *The investigation now in progress, ... to ascertain the origin of the Chicago fire, ... will, we hope, result in something tangible. Nevertheless, it must be admitted that very little satisfactory information has been obtained.*[2]

A significant portion of the questioning focused on determining the fire's cause. At the time, Mrs. O'Leary was strongly suspected of having started it. Daniel Sullivan was also considered as a suspect.

Following are excerpts from the official testimony given by three key witnesses: Catherine "Kate" O'Leary, Patrick O'Leary, and Daniel Sullivan.

Researching the Fire

Attorney and Chicago Fire historian Richard F. Bales spent years researching the Great Conflagration. He came to know the facts inside and out. In 2002, he published the book *The Great Chicago Fire and the Myth of Mrs. O'Leary's Cow*. The book provides a remarkably detailed study of the investigation into the origins of the fire.

Their stories, both individually and as a group, shed only some light on what happened either just before or just after the fire ignited. But no one claims knowledge of how it started.

The testimony is a matter of public record. A century later it was carefully transcribed from documents hand-written by writer Richard F. Bales for his book *The Great Chicago Fire and the Myth of Mrs. O'Leary's Cow*.

Each official point is indicated with a **Q** for the investigator's question and an **A** for the witness's reply. Witnesses were questioned for hours at a time. What follows are greatly shortened excerpts of their testimony about the fire.

Official Investigation

The investigation examined how the fire started and whether the fire department had failed to do its duty. Residents had their own opinions; they spread rumors that the city's firemen were inept.

The official investigations proved these rumors untrue. The fire department had done the best job it could with its staff and equipment. It had 185 firemen and 17 steam fire engine companies. A variety of smaller companies used equipment such as the hook and ladder and water hose.

The fire department's equipment was old. The men had been fighting fires all season. The deadly blaze on October 7 had all but exhausted half of their manpower. The raging fire was simply too much for any fire department to successfully battle.

In 1872, author Frank Luzerne defended the deparment in his book, *The Lost City!* He wrote:

Much has been said ... of the Fire Department. ... It has been hinted that ... the brigade, as a body, were utterly inefficient to accomplish their duty properly. A more gallant struggle against an overwhelming, all-powerful, merciless league of wind and fire, was never sustained by braver men who freely risked, and lost, life and limb in the terribly unequal fight.[3]

Testimony of Catherine O'Leary, November 24, 1871 Witness Number 5

In her testimony, Mrs. O'Leary said that she did not know how the fire started. She stated that she had not been in the barn for hours. She did not mention leaving behind a kerosene lantern.

Also, her testimony made it seem unlikely that one of her cows had anything to do with starting the blaze. The party she mentioned took place in the front of the house the O'Learys shared with a boarder. Surely, it would have been difficult for her to monitor the comings and goings of the party guests that night.

Q: What do you know about this fire?
A: I was in bed myself and my husband and five children when this fire commenced. I was the owner of them five cows that was burnt and the horse, wagon, and

Questions and Answers

The committee asked Mrs. O'Leary whether she had insurance to cover her property and livestock. The fact that she had no insurance made it unlikely that she would have started the fire.

Q: Had you any insurance upon your barn and stock?
A: Never had five cents insurance—I had these cows, one of them was not in the barn that night. It was out in the alley. That one went away ... My husband spent two weeks looking for it and could not find it anywhere in the world. I could not get five cents. I had six cows there. A good horse there. I had a wagon and harness and everything I was worth, I couldn't save that much out of it (snapping her finger), and upon my word I worked hard for them.[4]

harness. I had two tons of coal and two tons of hay. I had everything that I wanted in for the winter.

Q: Do you know how the fire caught?

A: I could not tell anything of the fire, only that two men came by the door. I guess it was my husband got outside the door and he ran back to the bedroom and said, "Kate the barn is afire!" I ran out, and the whole barn was on fire. Well, I went out to the barn, and upon my word I could not tell any more about the fire. …

Q: Do you know the parties who first gave you the alarm? Who told your husband that your house was on fire?

A: It was Mr. Sullivan gave the first alarm to me …

Q: Who is Mr. Sullivan?

A: He lives over there in De Koven Street.

Q: Opposite you on De Koven?

A: Yes sir, right across the road.

Q: What does he do?

A: He is a drayman. There was a party in the front of our place that night. I could not tell whether it was them made the fire or not. I didn't see it.

Living in the ruins of Chicago

Q: Have you heard from any person who was there,
anything in relation to anybody's going out to the
barn with a light?

A: Yes sir. I have heard of it. I have heard from other
folks.

Q: Who did you hear anything in regard to it from?

A: I heard from other folks. I could not tell whether it
is true or not. There was one out of the party went
in for to milk my cows. ... the first she told me she

mentioned a man was in my barn milking my cows.

Q: Did they state who the person was?
A: No sir. They did not.

Q: What did they want the milk for?
A: Some said it was for oysters. I could not tell anything, only what I heard from the outside.

Q: Had these persons in your house been in the habit of getting milk there before if they wanted it?
A: No sir. I never saw them in my barn to milk my cows.[5]

Testimony

A stenographer for the Chicago Board of Police and Fire Commissioners recorded 1,100 pages of handwritten testimony. He used a note-taking technique called shorthand. This system uses symbols to represent letters, words, and phrases.

TESTIMONY OF PATRICK O'LEARY
NOVEMBER 25, 1871
WITNESS NUMBER 13

Mrs. O'Leary's husband, Patrick, was also questioned.

Q: Do you know anything about the fire? Where it commenced Sunday night, October 8?
A: No. I do not, more than a man that never saw it.

Q: Don't you know where it began?
A: No sir. I could not tell.

Q: Whose building did it begin in?

A: That is more than I can tell because I was in bed when the fire commenced.

Q: What was the progress of the fire when you first saw it? How far had it burned?

A: It was my own barn.

Q: Any other building on fire?

A: That is more than I can tell because it was lighting so strong when I got up.

Firemen

Approximately half of the witnesses who were questioned were the firemen who fought the blaze.

Q: Just state what you did as soon as you found out that your barn was on fire.

A: Dan Sullivan is the first that called me out of bed, and I saw my own barn burning and couldn't get near it. I [turned] in and put the children in the street as far as I could. That is all I have to say about the fire.

Q: Didn't you do anything else?

A: Then when I had the children out, I went and was pouring water on my own little house until one o'clock at night.

Q: Do you have, in consideration of all the circumstances, any belief of how the fire commenced?

A: No sir. If I was to be hanged for it, I don't know who done it.[6]

Testimony of Daniel Sullivan
November 25, 1871
Witness Number 14

Daniel Sullivan had the most vivid recollection of the beginnings of the fire. He informed the O'Learys that their barn was on fire. And his story places him in the barn trying to save livestock at what had to be the start of the blaze. Does that mean he did it?

Q: Do you know anything about the origin of the fire Sunday night, October 8, that there was back of Leary's?

A: Just as I turned around, I saw a fire in Leary's barn. I got up and run across the street and kept hollering, "fire, fire, fire." I couldn't run very quick. I could holler loud enough but could not run. At the time I passed Leary's house, there was nobody stirring ... I

Chicago Fire

The complete record of official testimony about the fire was handwritten on 1,168 pages.

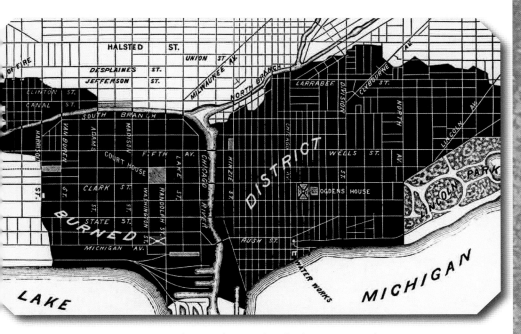

Map showing the area that the fire encompassed

made right straight in the barn, thinking when I could get the cows loose, they would go out of the fire. I knew a horse could not be got out of a fire unless he be blinded, but I didn't know but cows could. I turned to the left-hand side. I knew there was four cows tied in that end. I made at the cows and loosened them as quick as I could. I got two of them loose, but the place was too hot. I had to run when I saw the cows were not getting out. I was going along [the] right side of the wall. The boards were wet, my legs slipped out from me, and I went down. I stood up again, and I was so close to the wall, I could hold on to something and made for the door. Just as I got to the door, there was a ... big calf come along, and the back of the calf was all afire, and ... I thought it was time I got out of the yard, and I got out of the yard. As I got out of the yard, I had hold of the calf by a rope. The calf was all burnt. I stood and looked back at the fire as a dog will look when he is licked with a rope. I stood by Leary's house, and they were in bed. A man by the name of Regan came along. I was hollering and shoving in the door when Leary came out. He had nothing on but his pants and his shirt, and this is the way he done. He put up his hands and scratched his head same's he had a foot of lice in it. He went in and called his wife and she came out and just clapped her hands that way (indicating).

Q: Did you see any other building on fire?

A: Not at the very same time I got into Leary's barn.[7]

The Cow's Innocence Fully Established.

Of course, everybody has heard of **Mrs. O'Leary's Cow**, and very many people hold her responsible for causing the "world's greatest conflagration."

All must admit, however, that the *measure of guilt* attaching to the deed—terrible as were the consequences—depends materially if not entirely upon the *intent* of the animal at the precise moment when she gave the kick that broke the lamp and *upset* the good woman, rendering her powerless to extinguish the flames caused by the ignited kerosene. If, with "malice aforethought," the cow raised her foot, any Court in the land would convict her of "murder in the first degree;" but if from sudden fright, or any imagined necessity for *self-defense*, she was impelled to the act, disastrous as were the results, such "extenuating circumstance" should influence the verdict, more or less favorably in her behalf.

It is a well-known fact that Mrs. O'L., although having been much "interviewed" on the subject, has been extremely reticent, but, through a "chain of circumstances," it is now appears that she *has her own opinion as to who* caused the cow to use her foot with such force as not only to nearly annihilate the fair City of Chicago, but to shake the entire continent.

That "great events from trivial causes spring" is undoubtedly as true as if the sentence had been first uttered by Dr. Watts, or even by Anna Dickinson. "If what *has* been had *not* been, it is impossible to say what *would* have been," may have been the language of George Francis Train, or may not,—so long as the assertion is *true*, it does not matter whether Train or Horace Greely was the author of it, since the cow has already done more damage than she will ever be able to repair.

KINSLEY, of the "Emergency Saloon," on Michigan Avenue, where can be obtained a good dinner, and where are gathered a sufficient quantity of "relics of the fire" to stock half a dozen first-class museums, gave an order for an "Historical Painting," wherewithal to further adorn the interior walls of his "rough board" edifice.

L. V. H. CROSBY, that universal genius; who is probably the author of a greater number and a greater *variety* of "Songs and Ballads" than any other man in America, and who, through his compositions as well as through his musical performances, has been as generally known throughout the country during the last thirty years as any other man in it, is withal an *Artist*, i. e. a *painter* of rare merit, and to *him* Kinsley gave the order for the "Historical Picture."

Upon its completion it was copyrighted, and many thousands of Photographic copies of various sizes have been scattered throughout the country. ("Children cry for them—no family should be without one!")

The picture represents the interior of the O'Leary barn on that fatal October night, at the precise moment when the uplifted foot has "spent its force," but had not been returned to the stable floor.

The desperate cow, the terror-stricken and *upset* dame, the broken lamp still in the air, the ignited kerosene, the frightened fowls, the retreating rats, the bewildered cat, the scampering pigs, and the general consternation which prevailed, are all *vividly*, if not *truthfully* depicted.

A copy of this painting somehow reached **Mrs. Dr. Reid**, of Thomasville, Georgia, who has acted in the capacity of *amanuensis* for Mrs. O'Leary, and has sent to her brother in Chicago (**W. W. C.**, of the "**STAR UNION LINE**,") the following, which, it is believed, fully exonerates the cow. Mrs. O'Leary and "every other man," except the *artist*, who, it will be observed, is in some danger of arrest, unless he makes haste to make "the *amende* honorable."

MRS. O'LEARY TO L. V. H. CROSBY—ARTIST.

Arrah, ye spalpeen! it's meself that has seen
  Yer auld pictur o' me an' my antlsy,
An' there's proof in that same, the original blame
  Lies alone in yer own thavin' folly.

Sure a dacenter baste, the good Lord niver placed
  On the earth, than my crumpled-horn Durham,
She had niver been known, to burn up a fine town,
  Or commit other breach of decorum.

An' I knew she tuk fright, at some rare heythen sight,
  (The red fiend that gets up conflagration,)
I had iver supposed, till yer paintin' disclosed
  'Twas yerself—bad luck to yer nation!

How else could ye know, I'd a cat and a cow,
  An' illegant chickens—high perchin',
If yerself had not been, jist afore I come in,
  Through my barn for rich plunder a searchin'?

Then where jist outside, ye must sneakin'ly hide,
  An' the flames began scorchin' me nearly,
Faith! ye heard me exclaim it's *upset that I am!*
  But ye lost my true meanin' intirely.

I jist barely referred, in that terror-forced word,
  To my prospect of uttermost ruin,
An' I *niver* was known, in the *attitude* shown
  By yer paintin'—elewise a right true one.

For I stud on my fate, jist as proper an' straight
  As yerself or the Lord Mayor o' London,
Och! by this time ye know, there's many a one so
  I pret, as beroul themselves undone.

Ye may well understand, what I'm come to demand,
  Grant that same and again I'll be cheery,
But *foriver* I'll blush—till with paint an' paint brush
  Ye lift up on her fate—dame O'Leary!

If ye dare put it off, an' jeer, laugh an' scoff
  At this ginteel an' honorable warnin'
Faith, I'll turn on a blast o' High Sheriff an' Prosto,
  An' arrist ye—afore the nixt mornin'!

*The Cow's Innocence Fully Established, 1872: Mrs. O'Leary's cow
is used in a humorous publicity piece.*

Over time, the theory of Mrs. O'Leary's cow starting the fire was proved to be incorrect.

SUSPECTS AND THEORIES

The investigation and research of modern historians have cleared Mrs. O'Leary and her cow of starting the fire. While it seems certain that the Great Fire started in the O'Leary barn, no solid evidence explained how the blaze was ignited.

There were other suspects at the time and even a few confessions later. But the authorities never had enough information to draw firm conclusions.

DANIEL "PEG LEG" SULLIVAN

As noted in his testimony, Daniel Sullivan lived near the O'Learys. Sullivan testified that on the night of the fire, after visiting with the O'Learys, he sat for a while in front of the home of William White. It was there that he noticed the fire in the O'Leary barn.

Chicago Fire expert Richard F. Bales raised several questions about this part of Sullivan's testimony. Why, for example, did Sullivan sit in front of White's home? Why didn't he go instead to his own house after leaving the O'Leary cottage? And could he really have seen the fire from White's home?

Sullivan also testified that he ran to the barn yelling, "Fire!" But no one reported hearing him. Sullivan, whose nickname was "Peg Leg," had a wooden leg. While he said that he could not run fast, he also said that he had run from the White's home to

Valid Testimony?

Daniel Sullivan claimed that he noticed the fire breaking out in the O'Leary barn while sitting in front of William White's house. However, Sullivan would not have been able to see the barn from there. Another house would have blocked his view.

the barn. Bales noted that distance to be approximately 193 feet (59 m). Bales asked, "How could Sullivan hobble 193 feet into a burning barn that was full of hay and wood shavings, struggle with animals, and eventually leave, without being injured?"[1]

Sullivan's story did not add up. One theory is that he visited the barn to feed the cow that his mother kept there. This would not have been unusual behavior for him. In fact, Sullivan testified that he sometimes did this. It is conceivable that he knocked over a lamp or dropped a match while smoking. Then, as the fire spread, he rescued the livestock and warned the

Did a Meteor Shower Do It?

In 1882, scientists posed the possibility that the Great Chicago Fire resulted from a meteor shower. More than a century later, physicist Robert Wood suggested the same thing.

At a 2004 aerospace conference, Wood said that Biela's Comet had broken up over the Midwest in October 1871. The fallout, he reasoned, caused a meteor shower. The fiery pieces of the comet hit the earth—and the O'Leary barn.

Wood said this scenario could also explain why three other large fires near Lake Michigan occurred on the same day.

Named for the Austrian astronomer who discovered it, Wilhelm von Biela, the comet returned every 6.6 years. It was suggested that its orbit was disturbed by Jupiter, which broke the comet into two large pieces.

Wood theorized that one of those comets broke up into smaller forms and hit the earth as a meteor shower. The pieces hitting the ground would have been highly combustible. Wood cited several eyewitness reports that described "fire balloons" and fire falling from the sky during the Midwest fires.

O'Learys. Not wanting to admit to starting the Great Fire, he could have made up his story.

DENNIS REGAN

Dennis Regan lived near the O'Learys on DeKoven Street. He was also one of the witnesses in the official investigation.

Sullivan had mentioned Regan in his testimony. He said that Regan appeared at the scene before Patrick O'Leary came outside unaware of the fire in the barn.

Regan's version was similar to Sullivan's. Regan told the story of trying to save the O'Learys' wagon. He talked about trying to put out the fire. In order to try to extinguish the fire, one would need to be there just as it was starting. The timeline Regan gave for his actions in other testimony did not match up. He said he was there when the fire was still small. Yet if he ran to the barn when he heard neighbors talking about the fire, the barn would have been beyond saving at that time.

The Tale of the Cow

Years after the fire, reporter Michael Ahern made a confession in the *Chicago Tribune*. He boasted that he had written the first story about Mrs. O'Leary's cow kicking over the lantern. He said he'd made the whole thing up.

This claim was called into question, though, by others claiming they had been the first to tell the cow tale. To further confuse the issue, a former colleague of Ahern said he had written the *Chicago Tribune* piece under Ahern's name.

Another Possibility

Another theory is that neighborhood boys were smoking either in or just outside the O'Leary barn on the night of the fire. The assumption was that they panicked and ran away after accidentally starting the blaze.

Regan also told of hearing music from a party while running to the barn. All of the other testimony pointed to the party being over well before the blaze could have started.

Perhaps Regan and Sullivan knew how the fire started because they were in the barn together. But, this is no real reason to suspect foul play.

Lou Cohn

Louis M. Cohn was 18 years old in 1871. When he died in 1944, a press release announcing the settling of his estate included a surprising bit of information. The press release reported that Cohn was present in the O'Leary barn when the Great Fire started.

The last paragraph of the press release said, in part, that Cohn firmly believed that Mrs. O'Leary's cow had nothing to do with starting the fire.

> He and Mrs. O'Leary's son, in the company of several other boys, were shooting dice in the hayloft ... by the light of a lantern, when one of the boys accidentally overturned the lantern, thus setting the barn afire.[2]

Donations arriving from across the country for the citizens of Chicago

None of this information was ever verified. But it did bring up an interesting possibility for the cause of the fire.

MRS. O'LEARY: A FINAL OBSERVATION

Some people gossiped that Mrs. O'Leary lied about being in bed when the fire broke out. They said she had made up that story to avoid being blamed for the fire that destroyed Chicago. Who would not want to cover up a mistake that led to a tragedy of such magnitude?

The logical counterpart to that question is "Why?" Why would Mrs. O'Leary leave the barn after setting the fire—even accidentally—and go back into the house? Why would not she scream for help? Why would she risk losing her cows, the barn, and possibly her home without trying to save it?

The exact cause of the fire remains unknown. The extent of its damage, however, is clear. ⌐

The Chicago Courthouse and downtown area after the fire

Mayor Roswell B. Mason, 1871

A City in Ruins

hicago had sustained almost too much damage to comprehend. Lives and livelihoods were lost. Property was destroyed or ruined.

By Tuesday, October 10, Chicago was a smoldering city of devastation. The path of the fire had not distinguished between the rich and poor. Much of the prosperous city that had been full of life had become piles of rubble and ashes. The destruction and the loss of possessions, property, and lives were overwhelming.

An estimated 18,000 buildings were destroyed. Only a few homes in the area of the fire survived—including the O'Leary's cottage. In a nightmarish 24 hours, approximately 300 people died and more than one-third of Chicago's residents were now homeless. Those who had fled to the prairie or to the sand area of Lake Michigan had no homes to return to.

Message to the Citizens

On October 10, 1871, Chicago Mayor Mason issued a tentative, but hopeful, message to the citizenry. He provided information that would help maintain a sense of order. He also said, in short, that the fire was over and it was time to move forward.

Ashes and Ruins

The fire destroyed an estimated 18,000 buildings. Rebuilding would require time, money, and a lot of work.

Martial Law

With a city still clouded by smoke, the initial panic turned to anxiety. Mayor Mason declared a state of martial law. Generally, martial law is declared when a major event makes it temporarily difficult for a city to maintain law and order. Martial law puts the control of the city in the hands of the military. Lieutenant General Sheridan was given the responsibility to preserve peace in the city. He supervised the Chicago police force and the military members who came from states such as Nebraska and Kansas to help. However, the city soon realized this was not necessary and martial law was lifted.

Mayor Mason's Proclamation

"Whereas, In the Providence of God, to whose will we humbly submit, a terrible calamity has befallen our city, which demands of us our best efforts for the preservation of order and the relief of the suffering, be it known that the faith and credit of the City of Chicago is hereby pledged for the necessary expenses for the relief of the suffering.

"Public order will be preserved. The police ... will be responsible for the maintainance of the peace, and the protection of property.

"All officers and men of the Fire Department and Health Department will act as Special Policemen without further notice.

"The Mayor and Comptroller will give vouchers for all supplies furnished by the different Relief Committees. ...

"All persons are warned against any act tending to endanger property. Persons caught in any depredation will be immediately arrested.

"With the help of God, order and peace and private property shall be preserved.

"The City Government and the committees of citizens pledge themselves to the community to protect them, and prepare the way for a restoration of public and private welfare.

"It is believed the fire has spent its force and all will soon be well."[1]

HOPE AND ENERGY

News of the fire and conditions had

reached cities such as St. Louis, Cincinnati, Milwaukee, and New York City via telegraph. America's cities showed Chicago their support. People sent food, money, and essential supplies to help those who had suddenly found themselves homeless. More than $5 million in aid was donated to help the people of Chicago. Help was also on the way from England, France, and other nations.

At the mayor of Chicago's request, the Chicago Relief and Aid Society recorded and distributed the donations of money, supplies, clothing, etc. They took on the added responsibility of feeding the hungry and locating shelter for the homeless. By finding work for victims (such as clearing the rubble and saving bricks), the workers not only received wages, but their need for charity decreased.

James W. Milner wrote to a friend,

> *The general sentiment and feeling of the people is an honor to humanity. The businessmen are cool and cheerful. A quiet*

Children's Laughter

Chicago's children endured the terrifying ordeal of the Great Fire. Many lost the only home they had ever known and some lost brothers, sisters, and parents. Soon after the fire ended and all the adults started breathing sighs of relief, children were seen laughing and playing—trying to get back to doing "normal" things. Many adults marveled at the children's ability to smile in the face of such tragedy and uncertainty.

determination to accept the situation, and steadily weather it through to better times, is the prevailing feeling. [2]

TIME TO GRIEVE

As hopeful as the general attitude was after the fire, everyone needed time to grieve and process such a monumental disaster. In November 1871, Anna E. Higginson was still grieving when she wrote a letter to her friend Mrs. Skinner. She described the aftermath of the fire and the overwhelming sadness and loss experienced by all who lived through it.

I need not tell you of the greatness of the calamity which has fallen upon us. We can all feel that and most of us, I imagine, will feel it more and more as time advances. Men are full of excitement now and hope, the smoke of the battle has as yet not fairly cleared away—the realization, to be followed in many cases by depression and despair, will come soon enough. …To see the lines of rough sheds which are taking the places of all the magnificent buildings destroyed is simply

Struck Twice

William Ogden was a successful businessman in many ways. In 1837, he became the first mayor of Chicago. His fortune grew with his investments in real estate. Ogden recognized the value of a railroad system and was an important force in the building of several railroads. Like many people, he lost his home and downtown businesses to the Chicago Fire.

Ogden also owned land, a saw mill, a lumberyard, and a factory in Peshtigo, Wisconsin. On the same day as the Chicago Fire, he lost all of this to the flames of the Peshtigo Fire.

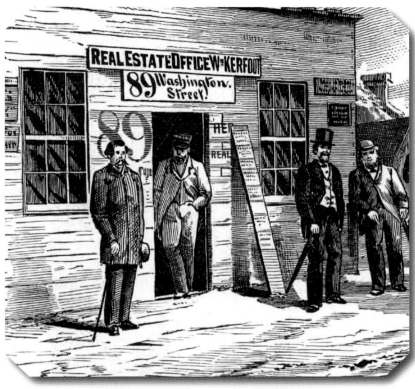

Fire victims prepare for the process of rebuilding.

heart–breaking. Chicago is thrown back now to where it was twenty–five years ago, and I for one do not expect to see it restored to where it was a few short weeks ago. The men of Chicago are heroes; their energy, cheerfulness and determination are something almost sublime; but I fear many a brave heart will sink under difficulties utterly unsurmountable.[3]

Symbol of Strength and Hope

The Chicago Water Tower was one of the few buildings to survive the fire. The limestone structure was built in 1869. It stands approximately 154 feet (47 m) tall. After the fire, it stood tall in the city as a symbol of strength and hope.

The nightmare of the flames of fire was over. The people of Chicago were definitely worn out and deflated after the fire. Devastation struck hard, but so did a positive spirit of hope and energy. Now it was time to tackle the job of rebuilding the fallen city.

Refugees living in tents

From the ruins of the fire, Chicago would be rebuilt into a great city.

A Bright Future

Many residents and businessmen feared that the fire signaled the end of Chicago. Instead, it became a turning point. It forced the city to examine its problems, find solutions, and start anew.

In a moving piece from the January 1872 *Lakeside Monthly*, William A. Croffut described the attitude he felt in the city.

> *From that windy nigh when the first prophetic flame shot into the clouds … till the last building fell and the destroyer had crept sullenly away … there was a helpless acquiescence on the part of spectators that was pitiful. But when the raging fiend had died … the old energy again came forth. … citizens who had cowered and fled before it in awe arose bravely and said, "We can conquer everything else."*[1]

RECLAIMING ITS FORMER GLORY

With the nightmare of the fire over, it was time to tackle the job of rebuilding the city. Even with the devastation, Chicago had a lot going for it. Chicago's prime location provided access to Lake Michigan and the Chicago River. The railroad tracks had survived the fire and could bring in construction materials and be an asset for commerce. Chicago also had savvy businessmen who realized the rebuilding of the city would offer even more opportunities. Chicago

Under Construction

Within just six short weeks of the Chicago Fire, more than 300 new buildings were under construction.

looked to cities such as New York for investors to help fund the rebuilding efforts.

In essence, Chicago was a blank slate. The city could now be divided into more separate residential and business districts. The area of the city had not changed, but the available space could be greatly increased by constructing taller buildings. The face of Chicago would change dramatically.

Not surprisingly, Chicago adopted new fire safety and building codes. Massive construction efforts made use of the latest materials. The building boom would establish the city of Chicago as the leading supporter of modern architecture

Not Totally Fireproof

The Great Fire is by far the most famous fire in Chicago. But there were other fires. In July 1874, Chicago had barely recovered from the Great Fire when a fire leveled 800 buildings and damaged 50 acres (20 ha).

On December 30, 1903, during a vaudeville show, the crowded Iroquois Theater suffered an afternoon fire. Faulty electrical wiring caused flames that killed more than 600 people. (The Great Fire of 1871 killed 300 people.)

In 1946, a late-night fire at the "fireproof" LaSalle Hotel destroyed three floors and killed 61 people. Someone carelessly discarded a still-smoldering cigarette, and a fire soon ignited in an elevator shaft. Sadly, many guests died after failing to react to calls of "Fire!" in the halls. Perhaps they thought it was a prank. By the time the thick, black smoke rushed into their rooms, it was too late to reach safety.

On December 1, 1958, a fire broke out in a Catholic school. The fire may have started in a basement trash can. It smoldered for several hours then spread to the stairwell and quickly gutted the building. The fire claimed the lives of three nuns and 92 children.

in the United States. With recovery assured, Chicago's position as the Midwest hub of trade and transportation would remain secure.

In a *Lakeside Monthly* article titled "Five Months After," *Chicago Times* reporter Everett Chamberlin discussed the city's road to recovery. He mentioned the many ambitious projects on the city's roster. For example, eight new railroads would arrive in the summer of 1872. The construction of new theaters, hotels, churches, homes, schools, and passenger depots was under way.

Chamberlin was proud of the city's recovery and accomplishments just a few short months after the tragedy. He knew Chicago was on its way to reclaiming—if not surpassing—its former glory. He wrote,

> "The shrewdest business-men of the West are all confident that in less than five years the commerce and prosperity of Chicago will be even greater than it had been previous to the fire."[3]
>
> — *Frank Luzerne*
> The Lost City!

> ... *if the stranger, having missed the sight of the most remarkable conflagration of modern times, would see a still-greater wonder, let him visit Chicago anytime during the coming summer, and see the work which has been done, and that which is in progress. Let him revel for a few days in the spectacle of what a young Western community can do in a single season towards building a great city.* [2]

Silver Floor

Reportedly, the floor of the barbershop in the luxurious Palmer House Hotel built after the fire was tiled with silver dollars.

Potter Palmer was one of the first to get started. His elegant and expensive Palmer House Hotel had perished in the fire less than two weeks after opening its doors for the first time. But he wasted no time in making plans to rebuild on the same site.

Palmer secured a loan of $1.7 million and hired the talented architect John Van Osdel. The seven-story creation was billed as "the World's Only Fire Proof Hotel." Completed in 1875, it was a major attraction in post-fire Chicago. Other major hotels to rebuild quickly after the fire included the Grand Pacific, the Tremont, and the Sherman House.

Recovery went so well that Chicago celebrated the "Great Rebuilding" in the summer of 1873 with a great Jubilee. From late that summer into the fall, the city also hosted the Inter-State Exposition in a magnificent building designed for the event. Made of iron and glass, the Inter-State Exposition Building stood at Michigan Avenue and Adams Street on the present site of the Art Institute of Chicago. The Exposition attracted visitors from all over. It showed the world that Chicago triumphed.

The total destruction in the burnt-out areas offered

The newly built Palmer House Hotel

an opportunity for new development and architectural renovations. In 1885, the nation's first skyscraper was completed in Chicago and towered over the city. With nine stories (and a hydraulic elevator) the Home Insurance Building dramatically changed Chicago's skyline.

Because Chicago was located on the shores of Lake Michigan, expansion

Magnificent Buildings

The designing and re-building of the city included architects such as Louis Sullivan and William LeBaron Jenney. Sullivan's assistant was Frank Lloyd Wright, who became America's most influential and famous architect.

A Fitting Location

Today, the Chicago Fire Academy occupies the former site of the O'Leary barn.

to the east was impossible. But with the innovation of steel-frame construction and large glass windows, Chicago could expand upward. These buildings would soar above the city.

Between the time of the fire and the dawn of the 20th century, Chicago's population grew from 300,000 to about 1.7 million. At that time, Chicago was the fastest-growing city in history. Businesses of every sort emerged in the city. And more people than ever before called Chicago home.

The Great Fire of 1871 was a grim time in Chicago's history. It transformed the lives of Chicago residents, yet the people survived and thrived. The fire also gave the city a lasting and special image as a place of renewal, progress, and great possibility. From the ashes and rubble, the people of Chicago turned their beloved home into the world-class city it is today.

The Chicago Fire Academy was built on the site of the O'Leary barn in 1961.

TIMELINE

1673	1770s	1795
Marquette and Jolliet explore the Chicago area and the Chicago River.	Jean Baptiste Point du Sable establishes the first non-American Indian settlement.	Treaty of Greenville, signed by the Native Americans and the United States, turns over the area that becomes Chicago to the United States.

1837	1860	1871
Chicago is incorporated as a city on March 4.	Republican National Convention that nominates Abraham Lincoln is held on May 18 in Chicago.	A deadly fire begins on October 7 on the West Side of Chicago.

1816

Treaty of St. Louis gives the United States control over the Chicago River corridor linking Lake Michigan and the Mississippi River.

1818

Illinois becomes the twenty-first state.

1833

Chicago is incorporated as a town on August 12.

1871

The Great Chicago Fire of 1871 and the Peshtigo Fire in Wisconsin begin on October 8.

1871

Lieutenant General Sheridan blows up homes on October 9 to slow the Great Chicago Fire.

1871

The Great Chicago Fire ends on October 10. Emergency supplies begin to arrive.

TIMELINE

1871	1895	1935
Official investigation into the fire's cause begins in November.	Catherine O'Leary dies on July 4.	Norman Rockwell completes his *Milking Daisy* painting.

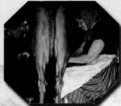

1937	**1960**	**1961**	**1997**
Chicago Fire is the subject of the *In Old Chicago* movie.	Chicago's Rose Bowl parade float features the O'Leary barn and a cow.	The Chicago Fire Academy is built on the site of the O'Leary barn.	City of Chicago exonerates Catherine O'Leary of starting the fire.

ESSENTIAL FACTS

DATE OF EVENT
October 8-10, 1871

PLACE OF EVENT
Chicago, Illinois

KEY PLAYERS
❖ Catherine O'Leary

❖ Patrick O'Leary

❖ Daniel Sullivan

❖ Mayor Roswell

❖ Fire Department

❖ Lieutenant General Philip Sheridan

Highlights of Event

❖ Chicago was very dry. In three months, Chicago had approximately one inch (2.5 cm) of rain.

❖ Chicago was one of the fastest growing cities. It was a city of wooden buildings and streets.

❖ Approximately 300 people were killed by the fire. More than 100,000 people were left homeless.

❖ While it was clear that the fire began in the O'Leary barn, it was never determined how the fire began or who started it. Mrs. O'Leary was exonerated.

❖ Despite the destruction of their city, the people of Chicago were determined to rebuild their homes and businesses. They regained and secured their position as the hub of trade and commerce in the Midwest.

❖ Chicago adopted new fire safety and building codes.

Quote

"What a sight: a sea of fire, the heavens all ablaze, the air filled with burning embers, the wind blowing fiercely and tossing fire brands in all directions, thousands upon thousands of people rushing frantically about, burned out of shelter, without food, the rich yesterday poor today, destruction everywhere—is it not awful?"—*Jonas Hutchinson*

ADDITIONAL RESOURCES

SELECT BIBLIOGRAPHY

Bales, Richard F. *The Great Chicago Fire and the Myth of Mrs. O'Leary's Cow*. Jefferson, NC: McFarland & Company, 2002.

The Chicago Historical Society. *The Great Chicago Fire*. Chicago: Chicago Historical Society, 1971.

Cromie, Robert. *The Great Chicago Fire*. Nashville: Rutledge Hill Press, 1994.

Sawislak, Karen. *Smoldering City: Chicagoans and the Great Fire, 1871–1874*. Chicago: University of Chicago Press, 1995.

FURTHER READING

Kyi, Tanya Lloyd. *Fires!* Toronto: Annick Press, 2004.

Marx, Christy. *The Great Chicago Fire of 1871*. New York: Rosen Publishing Group, 2004.

Murphy, Jim. *The Great Fire*. New York: Scholastic, 1995.

Robinet, Harriet Gillem. *Children of the Fire*. New York: Aladdin, 2001.

Web Links

To learn more about the Great Chicago Fire, visit ABDO Publishing Company on the World Wide Web at **www.abdopublishing.com.** Web sites about the Great Chicago Fire are featured on our Book Links page. These links are routinely monitored and updated to provide the most current information available.

Places to Visit

Chicago Fire Academy
558 West DeKoven Street, Chicago, IL 60607
312-747-7238
The academy stands on the site of the old O'Leary property on DeKoven Street. This is where the Great Chicago Fire started.

Chicago History Museum
1601 N. Clark Street, Chicago, IL 60614
312-642-4600
www.chicagohistory.org
The museum houses more than 22 million artifacts and exhibits to help you explore Chicago's past, present, and future.

Harold Washington Library Center
400 South State Street, Chicago, IL 60605
312-747-4999
www.chipublib.org/001hwlc/001hwlc.html
As the center of the city's public library system, it has a large collection of books and other works about the fire.

Lincoln Park
2045 Lincoln Park West, Chicago, IL 60614
312-742-7726
www.chicagoparkdistrict.com
Thousands of people fled to Lincoln Park and the shores of Lake Michigan during the fire. The city's largest public park features a zoo, beaches, harbors, and boating and sports facilities.

GLOSSARY

architecture
Overall design, form, or structure of a building.

bigotry
Intolerance toward people of different races, backgrounds, or beliefs.

cede
To surrender or give up something, such as land or rights.

chaos
Confusion and disorder.

commerce
Large-scale buying and selling of goods and services.

conflagration
Large fire that causes a great deal of damage.

contaminating
Infecting with bacteria.

cooper
One who makes or repairs wooden barrels.

devastation
Destruction or ravage.

drayman
One who hauls loads using a large horse-drawn cart.

exonerate
Clear of responsibility or guilt.

inferno
Uncontrolled intense fire.

inhabitant
A person who occupies a specific area or region.

innovation
> The introduction of a new concept or design.

inquiry
> Formal investigation.

mementos
> An object that serves as a reminder.

miller
> One who operates a mill.

recluse
> Person who withdraws from contact with others.

relief
> Financial help from the government.

scapegoat
> One who is unjustly blamed.

smoldered
> Burn slowly, often without a flame.

stenographer
> One whose job involves writing in shorthand.

telegraph
> Method of long-distance communication using coded electric impulses transmitted through wires.

testimony
> Evidence given by a witness.

unkempt
> Carelessly dressed or lacking cleanliness.

Source Notes

Chapter 1. The Myth of Mrs. O'Leary's Cow

1. "The Tribune Reports to Chicago on Its Own Destruction." *The Great Chicago Fire and The Web of Memory*. 30 Sept. 1997. Chicago Historical Society and Northwestern University. 10 May 2007 <http://Chicagohs.org/fire/conflag/tribune.html>.

2. Richard F. Bales. *A New Look at the Cause of the Great Chicago Fire*. 12 May 2004 8 Jan. 2007 <http://www.thechicagofire.com>.

3. Brian Wilson. *Wouldn't It Be Nice: My Own Story*. New York: HarperCollins, 1991. 156.

4. Richard F. Bales. *A New Look at the Cause of the Great Chicago Fire*. 12 May 2004 8 Jan. 2007 <http://www.thechicagofire.com>.

5. "Old Mother Leary." 6 Mar. 2006. NEIS. 10 May 2007 <http://www.neihs.nih.gov/kids/lyrics/leary.htm>.

Chapter 2. Chicago Before the Fire

1. Mabel McIlvaine. *Reminiscences of Chicago During the Great Fire*. Chicago: Lakeside Press, 1915. 37.

2. Ibid.

3. Frank Luzerne. *The Lost City! Drama of the Fire Fiend, or, Chicago, as It Was, and as It Is! And Its Glorious Future!* New York: Wells & Co., 1872. 90.

4. "Chicago: City of the Century." American Experience. 2003. PBS Online. 10 Jan. 2007 <http://www.pbs.org/wgbh/amex/chicago>.

5. Ibid.

Chapter 3. The Great Conflagration

1. "Chicago: City of the Century." American Experience. 2003. PBS Online. 10 Jan. 2007 <http://www.pbs.org/wgbh/amex/chicago>.

2. Ibid.

3. Ibid.

4. "An Anthology of Fire Narratives." *The Great Chicago Fire and The Web of Memory*. 8 Oct. 1996. Chicago Historical Society and Northwestern University. 10 May 2007 <http://Chicagohs.org/fire/witnesses/becker.html>.

5. Chicago Historical Society. *The Great Chicago Fire*. Chicago: Chicago Historical Society, 1971. n. pag.

Chapter 4. From the Eyes of the Fire

1. Chicago Historical Society. *The Great Chicago Fire*. Chicago: Chicago Historical Society, 1971. 11.

2. Ibid.

3. Mabel McIlvaine. *Reminiscences of Chicago During the Great Fire*. Chicago: Lakeside Press, 1915. 39.

4. Chicago Historical Society. *The Great Chicago Fire*. Chicago: Chicago Historical Society, 1971. 13.

5. Ibid. 15-16.

6. Ibid. 22-23.

7. Ibid. 27.

8. Mabel McIlvaine. *Reminiscences of Chicago During the Great Fire*. Chicago: Lakeside Press, 1915. 60.

Chapter 5. Landmarks and Businesses

1. Mabel McIlvaine. *Reminiscences of Chicago During the Great Fire*. Chicago: Lakeside Press, 1915. 40.

2. Chicago History Museum. 2006. <http://www.chicagohs.org/>.

Chapter 6. Investigating the Cause

1. Richard F. Bales. *A New Look at the Cause of the Great Chicago Fire.* 12 May 2004. 8 Jan. 2007 <http://www.thechicagofire.com>.

2. Ibid.

3. Frank Luzerne. *The Lost City! Drama of the Fire Fiend, or, Chicago, as It Was, and as It Is! And Its Glorious Future!* New York: Wells & Co., 1872. 90.

4. Richard F. Bales. *The Great Chicago Fire and the Myth of Mrs. O'Leary's Cow.* Jefferson, NC: McFarland & Company, 2002. 217-221.

5. Ibid.

6. Ibid. 234-236.

7. Ibid. 236-240.

Chapter 7. Suspects and Theories

1. Richard F. Bales. *A New Look at the Cause of the Great Chicago Fire.* 12 May 2004. 8 Jan. 2007 <http://www.thechicagofire.com>.

2. Anthony DeBartolo. "Odds Improve That a Hot Game of Craps in Mrs. O'Leary's Barn Touched Off Chicago Fire." *Chicago Tribune.* 3 Mar. 1998. 10 Jan. 2007 <http://www.hydeparkmedia.com/cohn.html>.

Chapter 8. A City in Ruins

1. Chicago Historical Society. *The Great Chicago Fire.* Chicago: Chicago Historical Society, 1971. n. pag.

2. Christy Marx. *The Great Chicago Fire of 1871.* New York: Rosen Publishing Group, 2004. 38.

3. 1. Chicago Historical Society. *The Great Chicago Fire.* Chicago: Chicago Historical Society, 1971. 26.

Chapter 9. A Bright Future

1. Mabel McIlvaine. *Reminiscences of Chicago During the Great Fire*. Chicago: Lakeside Press, 1915. 126.

2. Chicago Historical Society. *The Great Chicago Fire*. Chicago: Chicago Historical Society, 1971. 103.

3. Frank Luzerne. *The Lost City! Drama of the Fire Fiend, or, Chicago, as It Was, and as It Is! And Its Glorious Future!* New York: Wells & Co., 1872. 112.

INDEX

ABOUT THE AUTHOR

L.L. Owens grew up in the Midwest and studied English and Journalism at the University of Iowa before launching a career in publishing. She has authored more than 50 books for young readers and particularly loves to write informational books, historical fiction, and retellings of classic literature. Recent titles include *Pilgrims in America*; the Gold Rush novel *Tuckers' Gold*; and a graphic novel interpretation of Anna Sewell's *Black Beauty*.

PHOTO CREDITS

AP Images, cover, 3, 59, 79; Chicago History Museum, 6, 9, 19, 20, 29, 30, 41, 46, 51, 52, 54, 60, 71, 80, 93, 96 (bottom), 97 (top); Bettmann/Corbis, 12, 65, 87; The Bridgeman Art Library/Reproduced by permission of the Norman Rockwell Family Agency, Inc., 17, 98; North Wind Photo Archives, 23, 88, 96 (top); Stock Montage/Getty Images, 34; Oscar Gustav Rejlander/Hulton Archive/Getty Images, 39; Stock Montage, 42, 69, 72, 77, 85, 97 (bottom); Phil Martin Photography, 95, 99